The Good Vibrations Book

Lisa Buford

Copyright © 2017 by Lisa Buford

This book is a work of non-fiction. All rights reserved. No part of this book may be reproduced in any form, including electronically or audio without permission from

ISBN: 978-1976083099

Library of Congress Catalog Number:

Edited By: David Good

Typeset By: Write on Promotions

Photography, Design & Layout by: Byron Andrews for BAimaging.com

First Printing

Manufactured in the United States

Table of Contents

Dedication	i
Introduction	iii
Chapter 1	1
Chapter 2	5
Chapter 3	11
Chapter 4	17
Chapter 5	21
Chapter 6	25
Chapter 7	31
Recipe Introduction	33
Main courses	35
Snacks	72
Sauces	82
Breads	108
Desserts	118
Final Thoughts	135

Dedication

Forever grateful to GOD for my gifts - may my gifts always reflect the love and the glory of Him.

To my children, Tony and Tiffany, who have always been my inspiration - all that I do is for you.

And to all that read this book, and cook meals from it - may this book spread love and good vibrations to you and everyone around you!

Peace and Blessings!

Introduction

Have you ever wondered why the first thing a doctor tells a patient that has been diagnosed with heart disease, cancer, or most other major health issues - is to change their diet? And not just change their diet, but change it to a mainly plant-based diet? I'll tell you why, it's because doctors know the benefits of a plant-based diet, and they also know the damaging effects that processed foods, meats, and dairy have on the human body. They also know that Big Pharma is big bucks, and keeping people sick is part of their for-profit business. Real health care is found in God's garden - herbs, fruits, vegetables, nuts, and grains. The amazing thing about our bodies is that God created everything we need to heal and nourish it- but first we must stop putting the toxins in our bodies.

Although I'm not a doctor, and I strongly encourage you to check with your doctor before making any major changes, I have been eating plant-based foods for over 10 years and am a living testimony of all the benefits of this lifestyle. (I am 54 years-old, yes 54!) This book will give you insight into my journey to live a higher quality of life, naturally-no pills, no Botox, no fillers, and no surgery. There is no quick fix, magic food, or special drink you can take to be healed and made whole, you must go back to the basics, doing things naturally and consistently. Remember, this is a journey...not a race. Don't get overwhelmed at the thought of starting a plant-based lifestyle, just start from wherever you are- but start.

I'm here to help you along your journey, for that has become *my* journey - to help.

-Xo Xo Lisa B.

The Good Vibrations Book

Chapter 1
<u>My Journey</u>

    I get asked all the time, "How did you become a vegan?" The truth is, it wasn't just a simple transition for me. Over ten years ago I was suffering from my second bout of fibroid tumors which brought me to question my daily lifestyle. Three years prior to that, I had a very large (the size of a grapefruit) fibroid tumor removed thru myomectomy surgery. I was very healthy (I thought). I exercised every day, drank green tea in the morning, took my supplements, ate a low-fat/lean meat/no carb diet. I didn't eat junk food, no drugs, didn't smoke, only drank socially… the so-called norm. But the scary part of all of this is that I *really* thought I was healthy.

    I had the first surgery and the tumor was successfully removed and went right back to my "normal" lifestyle, not really thinking about making a change in my food choices. I assumed the fibroid tumor was caused by birth control pills (partially true), which I was not on anymore. I thought everything was great; after a speedy recovery, I went back to what I thought was a "healthy" lifestyle. But the second bout of fibroid tumors is what set all the wheels in motion for me to question everything I was doing. And all the answers being revealed led me to become vegan. After months and months of heavy menstrual cycles (so heavy I used two tampons and a maxi pad at one time, which had to be changed every hour), terrible bouts of cramping pain (kin to feeling like labor pains), and severe anemia (all this left me homebound for at least a week out of every month) - I was rushed to the emergency room where the fibroid had been living inside my uterus and growing like a baby. The tumor was the size of a premature baby and I was experiencing "contraction like" pains with blood hemorrhaging. The ER doctor (who was not trained for fibroid tumors) reached in and manually pulled out the fibroid that was attached by a stem to my uterus. (Imagine the excruciating pain of him pulling that out). He sent me home medicated and with a maxi pad. Eight hours later I continued to hemorrhage and was rushed to the emergency room at Cedars Sinai where my OBGYN was, and immediately I was told I needed a blood transfusion. The Doctors could not stop the bleeding and I was rushed to emergency surgery for a partial hysterectomy to save my life. The scariest time of my life because I was already under duress going thru a federal indictment (you will have to get my other book, Concrete Rose, to read that story lol). The stress played a big part in the growth of the fibroids, along with being on birth control pills for years (the estrogen) but I soon found out my diet was playing the biggest part.

    One thing for certain, the possibility of losing your life because of your health will have you re-examining everything around and about you. I was obsessed with finding out how and why I ended up with fibroids -

twice. I bought books, joined group chats, and Googled numerous websites. The one consensus as to *why* fibroids grow - was diet. Even though fibroids are more prevalent in women of color, and they are hereditary (my mother had a car accident very young and lost her whole uterus, both my grandmothers died when I was very young - so I had no reference for a health history of fibroids), it seems caffeine, dairy, poultry and red meat triggers the growth of fibroids. The growth hormones in dairy and meat (especially chicken) encourages the growth of fibroid tumors. Also, the estrogen in soy/tofu (which is in almost all packaged foods and boxed snacks) is a growth factor. The more research I came across, the more disgusted and disappointed I became with the food industry and FDA. I quickly gave up all meat including poultry (believing I needed the fish for protein) and became a pescatarian. This was just the start of a natural progression from pescatarian, to vegetarian (a few years later), to vegan to now *alkaline* vegan.

    The more I lived the plant-based lifestyle, the more everything naturally progressed to an alkaline vegan lifestyle. I share all this to encourage those transitioning in various stages, to keep going. This is truly a lifestyle and we should *always be learning and growing*. Even at this point, I'm still learning and growing, which is the beauty of life. So, don't get overwhelmed or feel like you've messed up if you slip back into old habits. There is no regiment or strict guidelines, there is just your own personal journey. Do your own research; listen to your own body; follow reputable vegan pages; talk to some vegans; try different vegan foods, and trust the process. Go at your own pace and compare yourself to no one, this is not a competition or a race. This is a process…learn to trust the process.

Chapter 2
Just Do It

    Starting - the key to every major life change you will have. But starting doesn't have to be overwhelming, starting can actually be exciting. Instead of thinking about all the things you will be giving up going vegan, think about all the things you will be gaining. You will be gaining true self-love. Eating well is actually a form of self-respect, and as you start shifting your eating habits, you start really self-loving. Everything in your life will start shifting to line up with that love as well. The higher you vibrate internally, the higher the things around you must vibrate as well. You will start to notice everything around you shifting for the greater. You will become (and I know this is cliché, but it's real) WOKE!

    Being *woke* literally means you're not asleep, eyes not closed, not unconscious... you become aware- aware of life. Things become more focused, more meaningful, more purposeful. This happens because plant-based foods are electric, it is the thing that triggers our entire body to function well. Plant-based food is alive, it fuels the body which is what food was created for. I think society as a whole has gotten off course as to what food is for; we eat for self (taste, smell, satisfaction), not for fuel (energy, right mind, wholeness). That is why we've been *sleep*; we've let the government and big companies feed us what *they* want to feed us (to keep us sleep). Now, the good thing is, things are shifting. Thanks to social media and the internet, we have access to useful information about plant-based foods and the benefits of eating them. We can easily Google numerous studies (which I encourage you to do), along with great recipes and restaurants to keep us on the right course. Trust me, on this vegan lifestyle, Google will be your best friend!

So now that we're woke, let's get started! I suggest starting simply by eliminating toxic foods that are easiest for you to eliminate - what would that be for you? dairy? red meat? packaged foods? Start the week by eliminating those foods that are easiest for you to give up permanently (because we are making this a permanent lifestyle change, not a *diet*). With each meal and snack, start replacing the eliminated foods with organic whole plant foods. Do not substitute with packaged vegan foods, they tend to have soy, wheat, and chemicals in them. (I'll talk more about soy and wheat later.) Each week add more plant-based meals and keep eliminating and replacing. Take your time, because you want this to be a permanent lifestyle change. The recipes in the recipe section of this book will help you along the journey. I will give you a rough outline in the next paragraph of what your day should consist of going forward. But the real key to transitioning to a vegan lifestyle is just simply - start.
(This is a <u>general</u> guideline for your day, this is not a regimen so you do

not need to stick strictly to this. This is simply a rough outline to help you form your <u>own</u> daily vegan choices.)

When you wake in the morning (adjust this to your schedule if you are on night shifts), start by drinking 8 oz of natural spring water at room temperature. This will gently start your body. Try to always drink room temperature water, it assists the body in elimination and digestion, especially while eating. I want to stop right here and explain why it's important to drink *natural* alkaline spring water and not filtered or osmosis alkaline water. Natural alkaline spring water comes from the natural spring, receiving all of its minerals directly from the source. Our bodies will always respond best by what occurs naturally, anything that has been manipulated by man is not going to be fully beneficial to us. As a matter of fact, studies have shown the long-term damage artificial alkaline water will do to the body. Think of artificial alkaline water as a "GMO" water, "you wouldn't eat a GMO food would you?". So why would you drink a GMO water? Finding natural spring water isn't as hard as you may think, most convenience stores sell it, you just have to research the companies- again, Google is your best friend.

An hour after drinking your water you can have your BREAK-fast, which is what the first meal is- a break in the fasting your body was doing while asleep. Your first meal should be only fruit or a fruit smoothie. This is a good place to add your hemp seeds, chia seeds, flax seeds, etc. The morning smoothie is just to get your digestive system up and going- gently. You will find that a big bowl of berries or melons is enough to keep you going for a few hours. Eat often, but eat whole plant foods. Keep organic nuts, dried fruits (make sure the dried fruits have nothing else in them, no sulfur dioxide), fresh fruits and natural crackers are all good snacks to keep with you. Stay prepared. The biggest obstacle is not being prepared! Always keep snacks with you! Lunchtime should consist of as much raw plant foods as you would like, and a small portion of cooked vegan food. They key is to eat as much plant-based foods in its raw natural state throughout your day, this is where your body will get maximum absorption of nutrients from plant foods. Cooked food loses some of its vital nutrients (yes, even cooked plant-based foods). So, with that being said, the more raw plant-based foods you can incorporate into your daily lifestyle, the better! Throughout your day drink at least one gallon of natural alkaline spring water at room temperature, and snack on fresh fruits, vegetables, nuts, etc. Dinner will consist of your one cooked meal- I have a lot of great recipes in the recipe section of this book, you can add or subtract different plant foods to the recipes, there is *no set* way to eat vegan- be creative! As you take this journey, you will see how enjoyable and satisfying vegan food is, let go of all the misconceptions of what you *thought* vegan food was. Think outside the box, start following as many vegan food pages you can on social media to help motivate you and keep you on track. Try new recipes, start a group cooking night, or initiate a vegan potluck at work. There are endless possibilities to making this vegan lifestyle change fun, delicious and easy breezy.

...

Lisa Buford

The Good Vibrations Book

Chapter 3
<u>Why Alkaline Vegan?</u>

I first encountered *alkaline water* when my best friend's sister was diagnosed with cancer and the doctor told her to start drinking alkaline water while going thru chemotherapy. The doctor told her that the alkaline water prevents the multiplication of cancer cells and can destroy or prohibit the growth of them. I further found that alkaline water is effective in reversing diabetes, preventing other diseases like Parkinson and leukemia by destroying free radicals. This information made me question the health industry, and why we are not given pro-active information- instead of re-active information. Of course, I started drinking alkaline water right away, bottles and bottles of high-end filtered water. If it was good for treating cancer patients, I knew it could keep me one step ahead, health-wise. But what I soon found out was that all alkaline water is not the same. Filtration water is basically a GMO (genetically modified organism), it has been manipulated by man to "mimic" natural alkaline spring water by being able to test at a high alkaline PH but lacking the important minerals (like magnesium and calcium) you receive from the natural springs. Case in point - you can just add baking soda to regular water to make it a high alkaline water, but it's lacking the important minerals from a natural spring source. The best choice is *always* what God created in nature for us. Always opt for natural alkaline spring water in Bisphenol-A free (BPA-free) bottles- again, Google the companies to see their bottling practices.

After researching water, I soon found out about *alkaline vegan*- a diet that maintains the alkaline balance in the body. This made perfect sense to me after researching about alkaline water and the benefits an alkaline PH of over 7.0 has to the body, it was only logical that this was the right path for me. So, I set out to research about alkaline vegan, and not just research, but put it to the ultimate test - my 30-day strict alkaline challenge.

Now you can't mention alkaline vegan without mentioning the amazing life and work of Dr. Sebi (please Google him), who brought to the forefront the information on alkalizing the body thru food and herbs. This has been documented in medical journals and thru Nobel Prize winners many years back- Dr. Otto Warburg (Google him) documented a cure for cancer by alkalizing the body (no disease can thrive in an alkaline environment). So, this is not new to the medical world, it's just new to some of us. But Dr. Sebi was certainly the one that brought it to my attention. I remember seeing Lisa "Left Eye" Lopez speak about this great man, and seeing the amazing transition physically in her. At the time, I didn't know his name, not until years later did I put two and two together and realized who this great man was. Dr. Sebi put me on the path of knowledge regarding alkaline vegan, he began to challenge my thinking and eventually challenged me physically. I set out to put his "theory" to the test by doing the challenge. The only way I could know for sure if this theory was true, was to actually give it the proper time and energy. Now mind you, I did a lot of research on why alkalizing the body is so important. Let's just start with the basics and not over complicate it, I'm all about easy breezy.

    The body's natural PH (potential for hydrogen) state is approximately 7.4 (average person). Alkaline compounds buffer acids in the blood with four main minerals that work together to keep the body healthy and running properly- calcium, sodium, magnesium, and potassium. The body works hard to keep the body in a natural alkaline state and will take from stored reserves whenever necessary to keep it balanced. That being said, why make it harder on the body to maintain its alkaline PH? Again remember, no disease can thrive in an alkaline environment- this has been medically proven and documented. After doing research on the benefits, I found no negatives to this "theory" so I was ready to put it to the test now. I have been on plant-based foods for almost 10 years at this point, but I set my mind to do a *strict* 30-day, Dr. Sebi approved personal meal challenge. I gathered the food list (which is listed in the next chapter) and set out to really put this to the test with my body. At the time, I had excessive mucus build up in my chest and nose every day, sometimes choking in my sleep from it. I had joint pain in my knees and hands from doing hair for over

Lisa Buford

20 years and suffered from tennis elbow because of the repetitive motion from hairstyling. I also was *extremely* fatigued all the time, I do mean *extremely*. I would literally fall asleep periodically during the day while sitting and even driving. I knew I was following a healthy strict vegan diet, but something was still off.

I started my 30-day challenge by following alkaline vegan pages on social media, gathering vegan recipes that I knew I could remix to make alkaline vegan, and started my journey. I wanted to give the challenge a fair shot, so I stuck strictly to the guidelines and food list Dr. Sebi approved. Immediately within two to three days, the first thing I noticed was the mucus was clear from my nose and chest, and the fatigue was gone throughout the day. Now mind you, I also was experiencing detox-like symptoms, headaches, and flu-like symptoms, which I knew was common, based on my research, so it wasn't just an easy transition. But each day got better and better and by the end of the second week, all joint pain was gone, I was mucus free in my nose and chest, and I was full of energy and sleeping sound all the way thru the night. I knew I had just unlocked something amazing for my body; I began taking a few of the recommended herbs and felt even more amazing.

Needless to say, after 30 days, I was fully convinced that alkaline vegan was for me. Again, this was a natural progression for me, and I'm continuing to grow and learn on this journey. The alkaline vegan lifestyle

The Good Vibrations Book

has also shown me that there are not enough food choices out there for us, most struggle with wrapping their minds around a strict food guideline. Eating salads every day was not an option for me (lol), so I started taking regular recipes and turning them into alkaline vegan recipes. I like food- a lot! So, I wanted to show people that eating alkaline vegan is not a sacrifice, the food is actually delicious! Eating alkaline vegan is not boring, plants are full of taste and textures that your mouth will love when prepared the right way, and even more importantly- your body will appreciate it.

Lisa Buford

Chapter 4
The Basics

This chapter will give you the basic information you need for an alkaline lifestyle. Don't overwhelm yourself, take your time and start by removing the toxic foods you've been eating, while incorporating as much of Dr. Sebi guidelines/foods into your daily routine as possible.

The Basics
No meat
No fish
No poultry
No Dairy
No potatoes
No corn
No canola oil
No tofu
No soy
No rice (except wild rice)
No wheat
No white sugar
No table salt
No microwaves
No Teflon or nonstick pans

Lisa Buford

No canned foods
No processed foods
No cooking in tin foil
No beans (only chickpeas)
No GMO foods
No hybrid foods
No manipulated water (including distilled, purified, and all artificially made alkaline water)
No pasteurized or from concentrate juices
No artificial sweeteners or flavors
No packaged foods (including vegan)

This is a *general* guideline to help simplify your journey, this is not a strict regimen (although I strongly suggest following the guidelines). Below is a complete list of foods that are Dr. Sebi approved for your alkaline vegan journey. Take this list to the grocery store when shopping and keep staple foods on hand for quick meals.

Vegetables

Amaranth greens
Wild arugula
Avocado
Bell peppers
Chayote (Mexican squash)
Cucumber
Dandelion greens
Garbanzo beans
Izote

The Good Vibrations Book

Kale
Lettuce (except iceberg)
Mushrooms (except shitake)
Nopales - (Mexican cactus)
Okra
Olives
Onions
Sea vegetables
Squash
Tomato (cherry and plum only)
Tomatillo
Turnip greens
Watercress
Purslane
Zucchini

Fruits

Apples
Bananas (the smallest ones or burro bananas)
Berries (all varieties- no cranberries)
Cantaloupe
Cherries
Currants
Dates
Figs
Grapes (seeded)
Limes (Key limes seeded)
Mango
Melons (seeded)
Oranges (Seville or sour preferred)
Papayas
Peaches
Pears
Plums
Prickly pear (cactus fruit)
Prunes
Raisins (seeded)
Soft jelly coconuts
sour sop
Tamarind

Lisa Buford

All-Natural Herbal Teas
Burdock
Chamomile
Elderberry
Fennel
Ginger
Raspberry
Tila

Grains
Amaranth
Fonlo
Kamut
Quinoa
Rye
Spelt
Tef
Wild rice

Nuts and Seeds (includes nut and seed butter)
Hempseeds
Raw sesame seeds
Tahini butter
Walnuts
Brazil nuts

Oils
Olive oil (do not heat)
Coconut oil (do not heat)
Grapeseed oil
Sesame oil
Hempseed oil
Avocado oil

The Good Vibrations Book

Spices and Seasonings

(mild)

Basil	Savory
Bay leaf	Sweet basil
Cloves	Tarragon
Dill	Thyme
Oregano	

(Pungent and spicy)

Achlote	Habanero
Cayenne pepper	Sage
Onion powder	

(salty)

Sea salt
Powdered granulated seaweed (nori, dulce, kelp)

(Sweet flavors)

Pure agave syrup (from cactus)
Date sugar

Lisa Buford

Chapter 5
Alkaline Vegan Tips

- You can use chickpea flour as an egg substitute for baking, just use one tablespoon chickpea flour and two tablespoons spring water to make one egg substitute.
- Sparkling mineral water is a great substitute for baking soda in recipes for baking.
- Never cook in tin foil or with Teflon (nonstick) pans, they leech heavy metal into your food. Opt for cast iron, glass or copper pans.
- Use silicone pans when baking or line pans with parchment paper.
- You can make your own plant milk with no straining. Use 2 cups spring water, ¼ cup hemp speeds, and ¼ cup date sugar. Blend in magic bullet. Store in mason jar and refrigerate. *No messy straining necessary.
- Soak your nuts before eating to help neutralize the enzymes. (Nuts have high enzyme inhibitors which make them hard to digest.) It also helps break down the phytic acid to help it get all the minerals properly absorbed. Soak in spring water (enough water to cover the nuts) with 1-2 tablespoons sea salt. Let soak overnight (12 hours), pat dry and place in a dehydrator or an oven on lowest temperature for

8-12 hours or until crispy.
- ❖ Never use microwave ovens, they are toxic to your food. Use a toaster oven or your regular oven on broil to reheat food.
- ❖ Eat organic fruits and vegetables only, it takes only 7 days on an all organic diet to remove 90% of the pesticides in your body.
- ❖ Apples are more effective at waking you up in the morning than coffee. Not just because of the natural sugar, but the vitamins in the skin of an apple release slowly throughout the body.
- ❖ Cilantro is a heavy metal detoxifier, Heavy metals in the body can lead to insomnia, chronic fatigue, numbness, burning or tingling sensation, muscle spasms, and migrating pain.
- ❖ Do not buy prepackaged lettuce (unless certified organic), they are washed in chlorine water 20 times stronger than the average swimming pool.
- ❖ Buy your organic staples in bulk form to save money, utilize local co-ops and farmers markets.
- ❖ Buy large quantities of staples online to save even bigger (they normally ship free over a certain amount of money spent). Join with a friend and order larger sizes together and split the cost (and the savings!).
- ❖ Buy your spring water by the case. You can save up to 20% by doing this at most stores.

- ❖ Go to local farmers markets on their last day there, just before closing to get the best deals. Most don't want to pack and take back produce.
- ❖ Eat your last meal at least 3 hours before laying down to give your body ample time to digest and rest. Only drink room temperature spring water after that. Also, first thing when waking, drink a glass of spring water to gently start your body to wake up.
- ❖ Bananas (Burro) are a great egg substitute when baking.
- ❖ Drinking cold water with food can cause coagulation and impede digestion, always drink room temperature water when eating.
- ❖ Sparkling mineral water contains up to four times as much calcium and magnesium as regular water. This can aid in lowering blood pressure.
- ❖ 95% of all chronic diseases comes from what you put into your body.

Lisa Buford

Chapter 6
Vegan Truth

There are several types of vegans. There is the junk food vegan, that just avoids meat and dairy, but eats all kinds of sweet salty packaged junk foods. There's the animal lover vegan, that won't eat or wear anything from an animal, but not necessarily eat only whole plant foods. Then there's the raw vegan, that only eats raw plant-based foods. Also, the alkaline vegan, that adheres to only plant-based foods that are on the alkaline side. And on and on, you get the picture. Now, I want to clear up some universal information that can benefit ALL vegans! These are "foods" (and I say that lightly) that should be avoided in your daily lifestyle.

Soy- Soy has the highest levels of phytoestrogens, probably more than any other food source. Phytoestrogens mimic the estrogen in our bodies. That might at first sound ok, but think about it. The leading cause of breast cancer, endometriosis, uterine fibroids and infertility in women is unopposed estrogen or estrogen dominance. An infant drinking the required amount of soy milk every day is taking the estrogen equivalent to 4 birth control pills. Men that eat or drink soy products have lower testosterone levels, this can cause lower libido, fat accumulation around the waist, loss of energy, stamina and virility and even man boobs (gynecomastia). Phytoestrogens are just one of many problems with soy and soy products. There's also protease inhibitors that can block minerals and proteins from proper absorption creating multiple health problems. Soy products also create thyroid problems due to the elevated levels of goitrogens, hindering the ability of the thyroid to utilize iodine correctly. Now does that sound like some sort of food or drink you want to consume? I think not.

Wheat- Wheat is probably one of the hardest foods to digest. It has been invented with chemical and genetic technologies to make it resistant to pesticides, drought, blight and easier to harvest. While they were tweaking genetics, they figured out a way to increase glutens for better "baking properties" (fluffier results); basically, you are eating fake food and chemicals- and you really wonder why your digestive system is full of gas and bloat? I'll pass.

Corn- According to the USDA as of 2014, 93% of all US corn is GMO (genetically modified organisms). Let's be clear for folks that say they would never eat this stuff but eat meat and poultry- most of the meat or poultry people consume is fed primarily corn. Corn is also the main staple in most prepackage shelf and frozen food (corn oil, canola oil, rapeseed oil, corn syrup etc.) Corn has been fashioned to withstand all pesticides and extreme weather conditions so that it can mass produce quickly with no loss to crops. Think about this- when you eat corn, it stays whole in your stools when you pass a bowel movement. Now what kinda food can withstand stomach acid that's as strong as battery acid? I don't want any parts of that kinda food! Do you? I think not.

Agave- Even though agave is on the Dr. Sebi approved food list, I still don't believe if he was alive he would approve it. I don't use it (if I do, it's sparingly). It has the highest fructose content of any other sweetener on the market, and higher in calories than table sugar. My preference is date sugar, which is simply ground up dried dates.

Vegan Packaged Foods- One of the most common mistakes people make trying to go vegan, is that people use prepackaged vegan food (especially frozen) as a transitional food. Most think it's a better option than meat, and although you might think that prepackaged food is a great idea to keep you on track, it can actually be just as damaging as eating meat long term. Most prepackaged vegan foods have loads of chemicals, oils, wheat and corn (as fillers) and toxic additives. If you read the back of the packages you will see a list of unrecognizable "vegan" ingredients. The simplest way to avoid all the toxins, is to only eat whole plant foods- Nothing boxed, canned, or prepackaged.

Canned Foods- Most canned foods loose almost all their nutritional value. First off, most foods packed in a can are full of preservatives to help prolong the shelf life of that food. Not only that, but the can itself is toxic to the food, even if the can is PBA free, it can still leech aluminum into the food. And if that's not bad enough, most companies utilize low grade foods for canning. Now who wants to eat that? Not me.

Yeast (including nutritional yeast)- Yeast causes the body to become acidic and is conductive to the overgrowth of Candida. Candida can cause everything from athlete's foot to extreme fatigue to body rashes. Even nutritional yeast can be damaging to the body, it can trigger itching, gas, and bloating (signs of your body not being able to digest it properly). Yeast is a fungus that resembles mold and gluten, both of which can bring on an allergic reaction. Now who wants that?

Vinegar (including apple cider vinegar)- Vinegar is highly acidic which can adversely affect your potassium levels, damage the digestive tract, and can cause stomach issues.

GMO - Probably the one thing almost all vegans can agree upon (non-vegans too) is that GMO's are never to be consumed. What's a GMO? A GMO has been manipulated by man in a laboratory to create a food that withstands pesticides and harmful weather conditions so that it can yield a larger crop. A GMO food can be spliced with DNA from bacteria, viruses, insects, animals, and even humans! The hard part about all of this is that the government does not properly label GMO foods. There is a Congressional bill in place to change this, and hopeful soon we won't have this problem. But for now, do your research on which foods are GMO and which are not. Buy only certified organic, which will cut down the chance of the food being GMO (but it won't guarantee it, unless it says "certified Non-GMO'"). It's up to us to do our own due diligence.

Lisa Buford

Chapter 7
You're Ready

So now that you're ready to take on this new part of your life journey, I've included some of my amazing alkaline vegan recipes in the next part of this book to make your journey even better. The following recipes will help equip you with food choices that will not only nourish your body, but will help keep you satisfied as well! Remember to stay prepared with as much food prep as you can make. Staples like spelt pasta, wild rice, quinoa, and bread recipes should be kept on hand already prepped and made. This will make those days when you don't have the time to cook a full meal easier, you can just throw some cooked wild rice in a cast iron pan with some alkaline veggies and voila! Stir fry! Make things as easy on yourself as possible- set yourself up to succeed. That means always having snacks on hand, whether its dried or fresh fruit, nuts, crackers or chickpeas from my snack recipes, or some of my amazing kale chips. Keep snacks on hand at home and especially when you leave the house.

And finally, to help make this next transition in your life into a wonderful experience, I hope you will incorporate the recipes in the next section into your daily lifestyle. Enjoy!

Lisa Buford

RECIPES

These amazing recipes are all made with love and gratitude. I hope you enjoy them as much as I enjoyed creating them. They are all alkaline vegan (you should use organic ingredients whenever possible) and easy breezy! I've created them with the mindset of making them economically friendly, time efficient, and simple to make!

Being a single mother for most of my parenting (and now a grandmother), I know how important all of that is. Not only will you love these recipes, but your family will too!

These recipes will bless your journey, no matter what stage you are at. Whether you are a long-time vegan, an alkaline vegan, just starting off as a vegan, or you just want to add some meatless nights to your lifestyle - these recipes are perfect for you!

Be creative, add them to your own recipes and put a twist to them. Remember - this is a journey, and the fact that you are reading this book means you are on the right path to living a higher quality of life. Enjoy!

Lisa Buford

Main Courses

Lisa Buford

Burro Banana Pancakes

Burro Banana Pancakes

2 very ripe burro bananas - mashed
1 cup spelt flour
1 cup sparkling mineral water - (more or less if needed)
¼ cup date sugar
1 tsp ground cloves
2 tbsp crushed walnuts
1 tbsp grapeseed oil
Avocado spray oil for cooking

In large mixing bowl add flour, date sugar, cloves, grapeseed oil and bananas. Mix well. Add water slowly to make a pancake batter consistency. Mix well and fold in walnuts. Spray avocado oil on pan and make small round cakes, flip once when golden brown on each side.

Chickpea Fritters

Chickpea Fritters

1¼ cup chickpea flour
1 cup spring water
1 cup crimini mushrooms - chopped
1 cup tri color bell peppers - chopped
1 cup kale - chopped
½ cup red onions - chopped
½ tsp oregano
½ tsp sea salt
½ tsp onion powder
½ tsp basil
½ tsp cayenne pepper
Grapeseed oil for pan frying

In large bowl add flour, water, oil and mix well (batter should be a little thicker than pancake batter, adjust with flour or water if necessary). Add all seasonings and mix, fold in all vegetables gently - do not over stir. Heat a cast iron skillet with about 2 inches deep of grapeseed oil until oil is very hot. (The key to pan frying is to make sure the oil is very hot.) Use a large mixing spoon and take a heaping spoonful of batter and place gently in hot oil, let brown fully on one side before flipping (insuring patty from falling apart). Place on paper towel after fully browned on both side to absorb excess oil.

Lisa Buford

Chkn' Strips

Chkn' Strips

5-10 large oyster mushrooms
2 cups quinoa flour
½ cup plant milk
2 tsp sea salt
1 tsp cayenne pepper
2 tsp onion powder
Grapeseed oil for pan frying

In two mixing bowls divide the flour, add plant milk to one bowl of flour to make a wet dredge (should be the consistency of pancake batter), add seasonings to wet dredge. Heat oil in cast iron pan for frying (oil must be HOT before cooking). You will have a wet dredge and a dry dredge- fully place mushrooms (one at a time) in wet dredge, then dry, then repeat once. Place in hot oil and fry turning one time until brown on both sides. Place on paper towel to absorb excess oil.

Cilantro and Lime Infused Quinoa

Cilantro and Lime Infused Quinoa

¼ cup chopped cilantro
2 key limes juiced
½ cup dry white quinoa
1 tsp sea salt
½ tsp cayenne pepper
Spring water

In large pot, add spring water amount to quinoa according to measurements on package directions. Add all other ingredients along with quinoa in pot while cooking so that ingredients infuse with the quinoa. Cover and let cook on low until all water is absorbed into quinoa.

Lisa Buford

Falafel

Falafel

2 cups cooked chickpeas
½ cup chopped cilantro
½ cup chopped kale
1 cup chopped red onion
¼ cup key lime juice
1 tsp cayenne pepper
1 tsp sea salt
1 tsp onion powder
1 tbsp. tahini
2 tbsp. garbanzo bean flour
*Spring water if needed to bind
Grapeseed oil to fry (or avocado oil spray to bake)

In food processor combine all ingredients (except water and oil) and pulse to a paste like consistency. Form small round balls and press slightly flat. Heat cast iron pan high with grapeseed oil. (Use enough oil to just pan fry.) Place small patties in oil and brown fully before flipping once, place on paper towels to remove excess oil.
You can also bake on parchment lined cookie sheet, spray patties with avocado oil and bake at 375 degrees for 20-30 minutes or until brown.

Jamaican Patty

Jamaican Patty

Filling

2 cups chopped crimini mushrooms
2 cups chopped red onions
2 cups chopped kale
1-2 tbsp grapeseed oil for sautéing

Filling Seasoning

1 tsp sea salt
½ tsp cayenne pepper
1 tsp oregano
1 tsp onion powder

Dough

4 cups spelt flour
¾ cups ice cold spring water
¾ solidified grapeseed oil

Dough Seasoning

1 tsp sea salt
1 tsp turmeric powder
1 tsp curry powder (optional, not on Dr. Sebi food list)

Pre-heat oven to 350 degrees. In large bowl mix all dough ingredients and seasonings, (except water) mix until dough becomes a crumble-like texture. Slowly add water until dough comes together, roll into a ball and cover with plastic wrap, store in refrigerator for 30 minutes. Meanwhile in cast iron pan, sauté vegetables (except kale) in grapeseed oil (1-2 tablespoons). Add kale last as it will just need to wilt down. Add seasonings.
Remove dough from refrigerator and flour down surface to prepare for rolling out dough. Take small batches and roll out, using a six-inch round bowl (or pastry cutter) cut small circles out, fill a heaping spoonful in center of dough, fold over and seal (push down edges) with edge of fork. Once all patties are made, place on parchment lined cookie tray, brush *lightly* with grapeseed oil and bake for 20-30 minutes or until golden brown.

Alkaline Mashed "NO Potatoes"

Alkaline Mashed "NO Potatoes"

3 burro bananas (make sure they are green and not ripe)
1 large shallot - chopped fine
2 tbsp grapeseed oil
2 tsp onion powder
1 tsp sea salt
1 tsp cayenne pepper (optional)
2 tbsp fresh chives - chopped fine
1-2 tbsp plant milk (get desired consistency)

In large saucepan boil burro bananas with skin on for about 20 minutes. Drain and remove skin, transfer bananas to large bowl. With potato masher, mash bananas and add all other ingredients.

Lisa Buford

Mock Tuna Salad

Mock Tuna Salad
3 cups cooked chickpeas
¼ vegan mayo (see recipe in sauce section)
¼ red onions chopped fine
¼ cup red bell peppers chopped fine
1 tsp dill
1 tsp sea salt
½ tsp cayenne pepper
1 tsp onion powder

In large mixing bowl, mash cooked chickpeas into paste like consistency. Add all other ingredients and stir well.

Mushroom Quinoa Burger

Mushroom Quinoa Burger

1 cup cooked quinoa
1 cup chopped bella (or crimini) mushrooms
1 tsp sea salt
2 tsp oregano
2 tsp onion powder
½ tsp cayenne pepper
⅓ cup rye flour (or garbanzo bean flour)

In food processor add all ingredients except flour (consistency should be like ground beef). Add flour a little at a time until patties can be formed, cook in hot cast iron pan with well coated grapeseed oil. (Make sure pan is coated well with oil or burger will stick.) Flip once burger is crispy brown (don't flip too soon or burger will fall apart) then brown crispy on the other side.

Lisa Buford

No "Meat" Meatballs

No "Meat" Meatballs

2 cups bella mushrooms
1 cup red onions
1 cup green bell peppers
⅓ cup fresh basil leaves
1 cup cooked quinoa
½ cup spelt bread crumbs (or spelt flour)
1 tsp sea salt
1 tsp oregano
1 tsp thyme
1 tsp cayenne pepper

Mix all ingredients in food processor until "ground beef like" texture, roll into small balls and place on glass baking tray brushed in grapeseed oil. Put under broiler on middle rack and brown until crispy. Once browned change over to oven temp of 400 degrees and bake for an additional 20-30 minutes. Pour your tomato sauce over and enjoy. (See my tomato sauce recipe.)

Pulled "NO pork" Meat Sliders (pair with dinner rolls)

Pulled "NO pork" Meat Sliders (pair with dinner rolls)

2 large Portobello mushrooms
1 large red onion
7 plum tomatoes diced (you can use roma tomatoes)
2 tsp oregano
2 tsp sea salt
¼ cup date sugar
1 tsp cayenne pepper
2 tsp onion powder
2 tsp basil
¼ cup coconut aminos
3 tbsp grapeseed oil
¼ cup spring water

Remove stem and gills from Portobello mushrooms, slice mushrooms and red onion thin and set both aside. In cast iron skillet, add 1 tablespoon of grapeseed oil and diced plum tomatoes, let cook down on medium heat. As the tomatoes cook down, use a potato masher and begin mashing tomatoes, continue this as the tomatoes cook down adding water (approximately 30 minutes). Keep mashing, as the tomatoes turn into a sauce, add the coconut aminos, date sugar, oregano, onion powder, basil, half the sea salt, and half the cayenne pepper and stir. Let sauce simmer on low for 30 minutes (add small amounts of water if necessary, and stir often). In separate cast iron skillet add remaining grapeseed oil and sliced red onions, sauté until translucent. Add sliced Portobello's and season with remaining sea salt and cayenne pepper; continue to sauté. Once mushroom mixture is browned well, add to the sauce mixture and mix together. Continue to let simmer on low for 30 minutes.

Quiche

Quiche

1½ cups chickpea flour
2 cups sparkling mineral water
2 tbsp grapeseed oil
¼ cup fresh chopped basil
½ cup chopped red onions
½ cup chopped arugula
1 tsp sea salt
½ tsp cayenne pepper
1 tsp oregano
1 tsp onion powder
1 tsp thyme

Preheat oven to 350 degrees. Mix all ingredients together in mixing bowl. Pour batter into silicone cupcake molds (or cupcake baking cup lined tin pan) Bake for 20-30 minutes until golden brown on top and able to stick a clean toothpick in quiche. Let cool thoroughly before removing.

Quinoa Thai Fried "No Rice"

Quinoa Thai Fried "No Rice"
2 ½ cups cooked quinoa
1 cup red onions - chopped fine
1 cup bell peppers - chopped fine
2 tbsp grapeseed oil
½ cup coconut aminos
1 tsp ginger powder
1 tsp sea salt
1 tsp cayenne pepper
1 tbsp tahini
1 tbsp date sugar
chopped scallions (optional)

In large cast iron pan, add 1 tablespoon of oil and heat high. Add red onions, cook until translucent then add chopped red bell peppers. In mixing bowl make sauce by adding coconut aminos, ginger, sea salt, cayenne pepper, tahini, date sugar, and remaining grapeseed oil. Add quinoa to onions and peppers, pour sauce over mixture and turn to low heat. Simmer on low while stirring occasionally for 10 minutes. (Use spatula so you can scrap bottom of pan if rice gets stuck.) Garnish with chopped scallions.

Lisa Buford

Spelt Waffles

Spelt Waffles

¾ cup spelt flour
½ cup sparkling mineral water (use fresh bottle)
1 tbsp grapeseed oil
2 tbsp date sugar
2 tsp ground cloves
Spray oil (avocado)

Pre-heat waffle iron. In large mixing bowl combine all ingredients (except avocado spray). Whisk all ingredients well (consistency should be a little thicker than pancake batter). Spray waffle iron with avocado spray before pouring in batter.

Street Taco (pair with Spelt Tortilla)

Street Taco (pair with Spelt Tortilla)

2 large Portobello mushrooms
½ cup coconut aminos
¼ cup chopped cilantro
½ tsp cayenne pepper (more if you like spicy)
1 tsp sea salt
1 tsp ginger root powder
1 tsp date sugar

Remove stem and gills from mushrooms, slice into thin strips. In large bowl add all other ingredients and mix. Add sliced mushrooms gently into marinade and let marinate for at least 1 hour. In hot cast iron skillet add mushrooms and marinade into the pan (the whole mixture). Gently sauté mushrooms on medium heat until brown. Pair with spelt tortilla recipe and add salsa and guacamole.

Taco/Burrito Filling

Taco/Burrito Filling

1½ cup cooked quinoa
½ cup raw walnuts (soak for 1 hour and drain)
2 tsp oregano
2 tsp onion powder
1 tsp sea salt
½ tsp cayenne pepper (more if you like spicy)
½ tsp ginger root powder
2 tsp coconut aminos
2 tbsp grapeseed oil (or avocado oil)
1 tbsp date sugar

Pulse soaked walnuts in food processor for a few pulses (don't overdo it or it will turn into nut butter). In cast iron skillet heat oil on medium - add cook quinoa, walnuts and cook until slightly brown then add coconut aminos (keep stirring with spatula so the mixture doesn't stick). Once browned add the rest of the seasonings and let cook on low.

Lisa Buford

Mock Tofu

1 cup chickpea flour
1 tsp sea salt
½ tsp onion powder
½ tsp cayenne pepper (optional)
1¾ spring water

Over a medium heat saucepan mix all ingredients to form a thick liquid. Transfer to a parchment lined tin spreading to about 2 inches thick and refrigerate overnight. Enjoy any way you would use firm tofu.

Lisa Buford

SNACKS

Lisa Buford

Burro Fries

Burro Fries
2 unripe burro bananas
Grapeseed oil for pan frying
Sea salt and cayenne pepper to season

In large cast iron pan add grapeseed oil about 2 inches high in pan. Heat very hot. (The key to frying is to make sure oil is very hot before placing food in oil.) Peel and slice bananas in long semi thin slices vertically. Pan fry until golden brown, place on paper towel to absorb excess oil, sprinkle with salt and pepper while still hot.

Spicy Cheezy Kale Chips

Spicy Cheezy Kale Chips

4 cups kale (tear into medium size pieces)- stems removed
½ cup tahini
1 tbsp date sugar
½ tsp sea salt
½ tsp cayenne pepper
1 tsp onion powder
1 tsp ginger root powder

Set kale aside. In large bowl mix all other ingredients to form a dressing. Massage the dressing into the kale to coat all pieces, (I suggest using small batches of kale at a time until all the kale is coated). Place in dehydrator – if you don't have a dehydrator you can use your oven set at its lowest temperature of 150 degrees. Dehydrate (or cook) at least 8 -10 hours until crispy. Let cool thoroughly.

Lisa Buford

Crunchy Chickpeas

Crunchy Chickpeas

3 cups cooked chickpeas
4 tbsp grapeseed oil
2 tsp sea salt
1 tsp cayenne pepper
2 tsp onion powder
2 tsp oregano
2 tsp basil

Pre-heat oven to 400 degrees. Drain cooked chickpeas and pat dry completely with paper towel. Place chickpeas in glass pan and cook at 400 degrees for 20 minutes. Remove from oven and toss in oil and seasonings, coat well. Return to oven and cook for 45 minutes to 1 hour, Remove and let cool, they will get crunchy once completely cooled off.

Lisa Buford

Hummus

Hummus

2 cups cooked chick peas drained (reserve a small amount of the water)
2 tbsp tahini
1 tbsp olive oil
1 tsp sea salt
1 tsp onion powder
½ tsp cayenne pepper
½ juice of key lime
⅓ cup chopped olives
½ tsp cumin (optional)

In food processor blend all ingredients except olives. Top with cayenne pepper and chopped olives.

Lisa Buford

Mushroom Jerky (bacon substitute)

Mushroom Jerky (bacon substitute)

1 large Portobello mushroom
½ cup coconut aminos
1 tsp cayenne pepper
1 tsp ginger
2 tbsp date sugar
1 tbsp grapeseed oil
1 tsp smoked paprika (optional)

Remove gills and stem from Portobello mushroom and slice thin. In large mixing bowl add all ingredients and mix. Transfer mixture and mushrooms to large zip lock bag and marinade for at least one hour. Place sliced mushrooms in dehydrator for at least 8 hours or until crisp but chewy.
*You can also place in glass cooking dish in oven at 150 degrees for about 4-6 hours. (Watch mushrooms so they don't burn.)

My "NO Peanut" Butter

My "NO Peanut" Butter
1 cup tahini
¼ cup date sugar
1 tsp sea salt

Mix all ingredients well, store in airtight container in refrigerator.
*You will never miss peanut butter again, and you will never endure a big mess trying to make your own alkaline nut butter.

Onion Crackers

Onion Crackers

1 ½ cups spelt flour
1 ½ tbsp grapeseed oil
1 tsp sea salt
½ cup room temperature spring water
1 tsp date sugar
1 tsp onion powder

Brush for top of crackers
1 tbsp grapeseed oil
1 tsp dried onion flakes
1 tsp oregano
1 tsp thyme
½ tsp sea salt

Pre-heat oven to 500 degrees. In large mixing bowl add all ingredients for crackers, mix well and knead slightly. Roll out onto parchment lined cookie tray and brush lightly with the brush mixture. Cut length wise and width wise to form small squares. Turn oven down to 425 degrees and bake for 12-15 minutes, watch so they don't burn. Let cook completely so they can crisp.

Lisa Buford

Onion Rings

Onion Rings

2 cups quinoa flour (divided in two bowls)
1 large red onion
1 tsp sea salt tsp cayenne pepper
½ cup plant milk
Grapeseed oil for pan frying

Slice onion into ½ inch sliced rings. In two bowls divide the flour. Add plant milk and seasonings in one bowl of flour and whisk well. Heat (approximately 2-inches-deep) oil hot in cast iron pan (the key to frying is for oil to be very hot) Coat one ring in wet dredge then dry dredge then repeat process once, and place in hot oil. Flip onion ring once until brown on both sides. Place on paper towel to absorb any excess oil. Repeat until all onion rings are done.

Lisa Buford

Mock Parmesan Cheese

½ cup raw walnuts
¼ cup hemp seeds
Sea salt to taste

In food processor pulse all ingredients until crumble like consistency.
*Use it on salads pasta and all your veggies

Lisa Buford

SAUCES

Lisa Buford

Bolognese Spaghetti Sauce

Bolognese Spaghetti Sauce

2 cups crimini mushrooms - half chopped and half sliced into fine strips
1 cup finely chopped walnuts
1 large red onion chopped
1 tbsp basil
1 tbsp oregano
1 tsp sea salt
1 tsp cayenne pepper
1 tbsp date sugar
1 tbsp dried onion flakes
4 cups chopped plum tomatoes
2 tbsp grapeseed oil
¼ spring water

In large cast iron pan heat 1 tablespoon grapeseed oil and add plum tomatoes. Let it cook down and begin mashing tomatoes with potato masher until you begin to make a sauce. Add basil, oregano, sea salt, cayenne pepper, date sugar, and onion flakes to sauce and continue to simmer adding water a little at a time (add more water if needed). Continue to let sauce simmer on low. In separate cast iron pan, add 1 tablespoon oil and red onion, sauté until translucent, add mushrooms and cook until mixture is lightly brown. Add the cooked mushrooms and onions along with the walnuts to sauce and cook an additional 5-10 minutes. Serve with spelt pasta.

Boysenberry Sauce

Boysenberry Sauce

1 cup boysenberries
½ cup spring water
2 tbsp date sugar

On stove top, heat all ingredients and let simmer on low. Cook on low until thickened, about 20 minutes.

*Pair with Burro Banana Pancakes

Alkaline BBQ Sauce

Alkaline BBQ Sauce

4 plum tomatoes puréed
1 tsp ginger powder
1 tsp sea salt
½ tsp cayenne pepper
1 tbsp date sugar
1 tbsp tahini
½ cup coconut aminos
1 tbsp grapeseed oil

Blend all ingredients together with whisk. Enjoy!

Tahini Dressing

Tahini Dressing

3 tbsp tahini
½ juice of key lime
1 tsp olive oil
1 tsp spring water
1 tsp onion powder
1 tsp sea salt
½ tsp cayenne pepper
½ tsp ginger root powder

Wisk all ingredients together well. Use for burgers, salads, or as a dipping sauce.

Lisa Buford

Tomato Sauce

Tomato Sauce

8 plum tomatoes chopped
1 cup spring water
1/2 cup date sugar
2 tsp oregano
2 tsp sea salt
2 tsp thyme
2 tsp basil
2 tsp cayenne pepper
1 tbsp grapeseed oil

In large cast iron pan on medium heat, add grapeseed oil and tomatoes. Let simmer, adding half the water. Mash tomatoes with a potato masher or large spoon while cooking. Add the sugar and seasonings and continue to cook down and simmer for about 20 minutes add remaining water. once cooked down transfer to food processor and pulse a few times (keep sauce chunky), return to cast iron pan to heat. (Add more seasonings if needed.)

Lisa Buford

Vegan Mayonnaise/Ranch

Vegan Mayonnaise/Ranch

3 tbsp coconut oil
1 cup hemp seeds
½ key lime juice
1 tsp sea salt
1 tbsp onion powder
Spring water for desired thickness

*For **Ranch**, add the following to mayonnaise recipe
1 tbsp chopped parsley
1 tsp ginger
A dash of cayenne pepper
½ tsp dill

Blend all ingredients in blender or magic bullet for 2 minutes.

Lisa Buford

Mango Dressing

2 tbsp chopped cilantro
1 large mango pitted and chopped
¼ cup key lime juice
¼ tsp cayenne pepper
½ tsp sea salt
1/3 cup olive oil
¼ juice from orange

Blend all ingredients in magic bullet or blender, add juice last to get desired consistency. (You can use thicker for burger spread or dipping sauce.)

Lisa Buford

Breads

Dinner Rolls/Mini Burger Buns

Dinner Rolls/Mini Burger Buns

½ cup rye flour
½ cup spelt flour
¾ cup sparkling mineral water
1 tsp sea salt
1 tbsp date sugar (or 2 tsp agave)
1 tbsp grapeseed oil
Sesame seeds to top

Pre-heat oven to 350 degrees. In mixing bowl, mix all ingredients except sesame seeds (this will be a wet dough). Pour into silicone molds or lined cupcake tins and sprinkle with sesame seeds. Bake for 25 minutes or until slightly brown on top, cool completely before removing from mold or pan to avoid sticking.

Foccaccia Bread

Foccaccia Bread

Bread

½ cup spelt flour
½ cup rye flour
¾ sparkling mineral water
½ tsp sea salt
1 tbsp grapeseed oil

Bread Brush Mixture

3 tbsp grapeseed oil
1 tsp sea salt
1 tsp cayenne pepper
1 tsp oregano
1 tsp basil
1 tsp thyme

Pre-heat oven to 400 degrees. In large bowl, mix all bread ingredients together. With spatula, spread bread mixture out onto parchment lined cookie tray making two large circles (mixture will be slightly tacky). In small bowl, mix all the bread brush mixture together, lightly brush top of bread with mixture before baking. Bake for 20 minutes, turning pan once half way thru.

Socca

Socca

1 cup garbanzo bean flour
1 cup plus 1 tbsp spring water
1½ tbsp grapeseed oil
1 tsp sea salt
1 tsp turmeric (optional)

Mix all ingredients in large bowl, whisk well. Pour thin coat (like a pancake) in lightly brushed (with grapeseed oil) cast iron pan. Place in pre-heated *broiler* (not on oven setting, on broiler setting), cook until very brown on top (approximately 20 minutes, but watch it).

Spelt Torillas

Spelt Tortillas
1 cup spelt flour
½ cup spring water
1 tbsp grapeseed oil
½ tsp sea salt

Mix all ingredients in bowl, roll into a ball and let sit in refrigerator for 20 minutes. Heat cast iron pan, roll dough into small balls and rollout flat tortillas. Cook in cast iron pan (no oil needed), flip once.

Lisa Buford

Desserts

Banana Muffins

Banana Muffins

1½ cup garbanzo bean flour
½ cup sparkling mineral water (make sure it's a fresh bottle)
2 very ripe burro bananas
¾ cup date sugar
¼ cup grapeseed oil
1 tbsp sea moss gel

Mash bananas well, in separate bowl add all other ingredients and then add in bananas and mix gently, do not over stir batter. Pour into lined cupcake tins or use silicone molds and bake in pre-heated 350-degree oven for 20-25 minutes or until lightly brown on top. Let cool before removing.

Berry Crumble Pie

Berry Crumble Pie

Crumble

⅓ cup grapeseed oil
½ cup date sugar
1 cup kamut flour
1 tbsp plant milk

Fruit filling

2 cups peaches (chopped into small chunks)
1 cup boysenberries
1 tbsp date sugar

Pre-heat oven to 375 degrees. In large bowl toss fruit with sugar. In mixing bowl mix all crumble ingredients together to form crumble topping (mixture will be like wet crumbled sand). Pour fruit mixture into (3) one cup small baking cups. Top with crumble. DO NOT MIX. Bake for 20-30 minutes or until topping turns golden brown. Let cool completely.

Lisa Buford

Blueberry Muffins

Blueberry Muffins

1 cup chickpea flour
⅔ cup spelt flour
1 cup sparkling mineral water
⅔ cup date sugar
2 tbsp grapeseed oil
½ tsp sea salt
1 tsp ground cloves
1 cup fresh blueberries

Pre heat oven to 350-degrees. Mix all ingredients (except blueberries) in mixing bowl, fold in blueberries gently. In muffin pan, lined with cupcake paper, pour batter to fill each muffin. Bake for 25-30 minutes or until lightly golden brown.

Cast Iron Peach Cobbler Cake

Cast Iron Peach Cobbler Cake

Filling

2½ cups fresh peaches, peeled and chopped
1 tbsp kamut flour
½ cup spring water
½ cup date sugar

Cake batter

1 tbsp grapeseed oil
1½ cup kamut flour
1½ cup sparkling mineral water
½ cup date sugar

On stove top, heat filling mixture in pot, let simmer on low until mixture thickens. Pre-heat oven to 350 degrees. Mix crust batter in large bowl, pour batter into lightly greased cast iron skillet, pour filling on top of batter in center. DO NOT MIX THEM TOGETHER. Bake at 350 degrees for 30-40 minutes.

Old Fashion Donuts

Old Fashion Donuts

1 cup spelt flour
½ cup teff flour
½ tsp salt
½ cup date sugar
½ cup agave
½ cup grapeseed oil
½ tsp ginger powder
½ tsp allspice
½ tsp ground clove
3 tbsp aquafaba

Preheat oven to 350 degrees. In large mixing bowl mix all ingredients together. Pour into silicone donut molds and bake for 15-20 minutes or until golden brown.

Fig Bars

Fig Bars

Dough
2 tbsp grapeseed oil
¾ cup spelt flour
¼ teff flour
1 tsp clove
¼ tsp sea salt
2 tbsp coconut nectar (or agave)
2 tbsp date sugar
⅓ cup spring water

Filling
12-14 dried figs (I used the light figs)
1 tbsp spring water
*plus, spring water for soaking figs

Pre-heat oven to 375 degrees. In small bowl let figs soak for 30 minutes in water. Meanwhile in mixing bowl mix all dough ingredients, roll into ball and cover with plastic wrap, store in refrigerator while making filling. Drain figs, pulse in food processor with 1 tablespoon spring water until paste forms. Roll out dough in long formation (approximately 12 inches by 5 inches), place mixture evenly down middle center length wise (the 12 inch way) and fold dough over width wise to form a center seam, close seam with warm water (it will look like a log shape). Flip log over and bake seam side down on parchment lined cookie tray for 15 minutes. Let cool fully, slice into 2 inch wide cookies.

Lisa Buford

Peach Cobbler

Peach Cobbler

Filling

2½ cups fresh peaches peeled and chopped
1 tsp ground cloves
1 tbsp Kamut flour
½ cup spring water
½ cup date sugar
1 tbsp coconut nectar (or agave)

Crust

1⅓ cup Kamut flour
½ tsp sea salt
⅓ cup grapeseed oil (solidified in refrigerator)
⅔ cup plant milk
⅓ cup date sugar

Pre-heat oven to 350 degrees. On stove top add all filling mixture, let thicken on low temperature. Meanwhile in large bowl make crust dough. Add flour, sea salt, sugar, and then add oil to form a crumble mixture. Slowly add in milk to form dough. Roll into ball, wrap in plastic wrap and store in refrigerator for 1 hour (this is important step, so dough can settle and not fall apart when rolling out). Roll out dough onto flour dusted surface to form bottom crust. Line crust in square glass pan, add peach mixture. Roll out dough for top crust, add on top of peach mixture. Brush top crust with plant milk and bake for 30 minutes or until crust is golden brown.

Walnut Tahini Cookies

Walnut Tahini Cookies

1 cup spelt flour
1 cup sparkling mineral water
3 tbsp tahini butter
2 tbsp Irish sea moss gel (or 2 tbsp natural apple sauce)
½ cup currants
1 tsp sea salt
½ cup sprouted walnuts
1 tsp ground cloves
1 tbsp grapeseed oil
¾ date sugar

Pre heat oven to 350 degrees. In large bowl mix all ingredients (it will be slightly wet) scoop heaping spoonful onto parchment lined cookie tray. Bake for 20 minutes or until golden brown, let cool fully before removing from parchment paper.

Lisa Buford

Final Thoughts

As you go forward on your vegan journey, I encourage you to share this book, the recipes and even your cooked meals! You have all the tools needed to start (or stay the course) on your vegan journey. Don't get overwhelmed or beat yourself up if you stray off course; just get back on track with some of the great recipes in this book.

Remember –this is not a race, do NOT compare yourself to anyone. Take your time, enjoy the journey, and trust the process….

Made in the USA
Lexington, KY
27 November 2017